AMERICAN HORTICULTURAL SOCIETY
PRACTICAL GUIDES

PATHS &
PAVING

AMERICAN HORTICULTURAL SOCIETY
PRACTICAL GUIDES

PATHS &
PAVING

DK PUBLISHING, INC.
www.dk.com

A DK PUBLISHING BOOK
www.dk.com

SERIES EDITOR Pamela Brown
SERIES ART EDITOR Stephen Josland
DESIGNER Alison Donovan
US EDITOR Ray Rogers

MANAGING EDITOR Louise Abbott
MANAGING ART EDITOR Lee Griffiths

DTP DESIGNER Matthew Greenfield

PRODUCTION Ruth Charlton, Mandy Inness

First American Edition, 1999
2 4 6 8 10 9 7 5 3

Published in the United States by
DK Publishing, Inc., 95 Madison Avenue, New York, New York 10016

ISBN 0–7894–4158–6

Reproduced by Colourscan, Singapore
Printed and bound by Star Standard Industries, Singapore

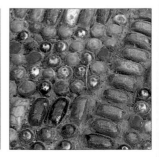

CONTENTS

PATHS AND PAVING IN THE GARDEN 7

Making hard surfaces practical yet attractive; routing
paths and siting paving; choosing the most suitable
materials and adding decorative detail.

LAYING PATHS AND SURFACES 23

How to prepare the ground and lay a variety of
surfaces using materials to suit your style;
useful ideas for finishing touches.

GETTING DOWN TO BASICS 64

Practical advice on choosing and sourcing materials;
buying in quantity; tools to buy and to rent; safety while
you work; maintaining paths and surfaces.

PATHS AND PAVING IN THE GARDEN

WHY USE HARD SURFACES?

EVERY GARDENER KNOWS THE VALUE of soil and also understands that the best place for it is in the garden, not on shoes. The practical advantages of hard surfaces are the first reason why paths crisscross our properties – but then we realize that, with the huge range of materials and effects available, they can enhance our garden designs and plantings and be beautiful in their own right.

EASY ACCESS

Hard surfaces make it easy to get around the garden, whether it is simply from the driveway to the house door or through the borders and down to the compost pile. At the most basic level they provide clean, all-weather access to any part of the garden. If carefully chosen, they also look decorative and can be planned to blend with and enhance the materials, color, and style of surrounding buildings or nearby planting; a stone or gravel path, for example, would fit in well with a rock garden. For those for whom gardening is a chore, not a passion, hard surfaces are a labor-saving way to cover ground. They do not preclude color from plants, because these can be grown in containers and raised beds.

▶ DEFINING A ROUTE
Using attractive and sympathetic materials to provide a little variation on the quickest route from A to B makes this path a strong design element, linking the house and garden in a most satisfying way.

◀ PERFECT PAVING
A paved area provides all-weather access and a neutral, light-reflective base color that is a perfect foil for this low-maintenance planting.

ARCHITECTURAL FRAMEWORK

Whatever the style of your garden, hard materials make up a structural framework for its design. They provide an architectural "skeleton" that underlies, frames, and enhances softer elements provided by plantings. And while all hard materials need to be functional and durable, you should bear in mind that they represent the single most important element in linking house and yard. As such, hard surfaces will provide the most aesthetic pleasure if you choose materials that blend, match, or contrast with the materials used in the house.

CHANGING LEVELS

The use of hard landscaping to create different levels introduces an added element of interest and allows features or focal points to be seen from more than one angle. A sloping site can be laid out as a succession of gentle gradients, either with sweeping paths or terraces. Terrace beds can be retained with low walls or wood, using slopes or steps to link them. Wide steps can be used to display pots, while narrow, meandering steps between tall plantings create an air of mystery – the lure of something hidden just around the corner.

STEPS AND PAVING
Where space does not permit a gentle gradient, a series of steps securely built from hard landscaping materials are essential to make changes in level safely negotiable. Carefully planned steps can also provide an irresistible lure to explore hidden features or, conversely, they may offer the potential for a series of views from different heights over the remainder of the area.

◄ ADAPTABLE GRAVEL
Loose materials such as gravel are practical, economical, and stylish, blending well with a wide range of other materials, such as cobblestones and decking.

▼ FORMAL PATTERN
Even flat and level areas can be given definition and interest by laying simple paving materials (here brick) in imaginative ways and introducing slight changes of level.

PLACES TO PAUSE

Narrow, straight paths are often purely functional routes to get from one point to another, but when they open out into a broader area, the natural reaction is to pause and look at the surroundings. Here is an opportunity to be adventurous and to combine different types of surface. A rough-textured surface, for example,

> ### Use color or texture to define different parts of an area

can be used to slow the pace naturally and signal an opportunity to enjoy a vista that has opened up before you. A variation in color or texture can also be exploited as a visual marker. Use it to proclaim a change in level or direction or to define a separation between different areas of the garden, thus creating the boundaries of a succession of garden "rooms."

EASY MAINTENANCE

In comparison to a grass path, most hard surfaces represent considerable investment in time and money, but the long-term advantage is that once laid, most require minimal effort to keep them neat. Usually all that is needed is an occasional sweep or a scrub to remove algal growth that may have accumulated in wet weather. Wooden decking needs regular applications of stain or preservative to extend its life and to keep it looking pristine.

SITING A PAVED AREA

THE SITING OF A PAVED AREA depends largely on its proposed purpose, and its function will also dictate the most suitable materials. It makes sense, for example, to site a patio for dining and entertaining within easy reach of the kitchen door or to place an area for repose and quiet relaxation in a secluded place away from hustle and bustle. The materials used should be chosen to withstand the expected amount of traffic or wear and tear.

SIZE AND SHAPE

While the shape of a paved area is largely a matter of taste, it is important to consider whether the shape you desire can easily be constructed in the material of your choice without complicated cutting to fit. An area whose outline is composed of straight edges or long, sweeping curves is not only the easiest to construct, it is also the most likely to confer an elegant simplicity to the overall design.

PATIO FOR OUTDOOR LIVING
It makes sense to site a patio for dining within easy reach of a door. Here, honey-toned pavers brighten without reflective glare.

Perhaps the most important factor to consider is the dimensions. It is easy to make such areas too small, partly because the human eye perceives scale differently indoors and out. Paved areas need to be large enough to allow for comfortable, unrestricted movement, whatever activities you propose for the site. For example, a minimum width of 6½ft/2m is essential to permit comfortable seating around a dining table. This must obviously be larger if you also wish to incorporate other features such as a barbecue. And if you wish to decorate areas with pots, planters, or other garden furniture, surfaces need to be clear of clutter that may cause accidents.

A SECLUDED NICHE
*In shade, lead the way to secluded areas with
a path that can easily be kept clear of slippery
mud, mosses, and algae.*

SITING IN SUN OR SHADE

In summer, a shady sitting area is a cooling
refuge from the heat of the day, particularly
if surrounded by lush foliage. But in deep
shade, damp surfaces are prone to algal
and moss growth, especially in spring,

> Dark-stained wood
> is visually sympathetic
> in shady areas

so the material used must be easy to clean.
Rough-textured materials will become
attractively mossy without danger of
accidents, but glossy surfaces, such as tiles,
should be avoided. Dark-stained wood is
sympathetic in shade but needs regular
treatment with a wood preservative to
eliminate slippery mosses.

Most common materials are suitable for
sunny areas. Stone and paving reflect heat
and can make a sun trap in summer, yet
they remain pleasant and accessible in
winter. Surface texture is seen most clearly
in sun, and any patternwork will be greatly
enhanced. Bear in mind that light-colored
materials reflect glare uncomfortably in
bright sun; soft tones of earthy gold or dove
gray lighten without such harsh reflectivity.

SECURITY ASPECTS

Pots, ornaments, and garden furniture left
out overnight can be a security worry, but
you can take steps to reduce the risks:
• Secure pots, barrels, and garden benches
with bolts set in concrete or between slabs.
• Grow plants in sunken pots between the
paving or in large, heavy barrels that are not
easily lifted.
• Use gravel or stone chips to provide a noisy
deterrent underfoot.
• Install garden lighting for security and to
enhance the area at night.
• Avoid screening with tall plants, which can
provide cover for intruders.

ROUTING THE PATH

Paths are routes for travel, and there is little point linking two places where no one wants to walk. Before starting, identify the most traveled routes on your property, then use these as a basis for the plan. Look at aesthetic considerations, and adapt routes to accommodate the shapes of lawns and borders and to give views through the area. A formal plan will require straight tracks that bisect the area, while an informal design can have intricately twisting paths.

GETTING FROM A TO B

When planning paths for practical, all-weather access, it is important to choose a surface that is easy to walk on. This may be something as simple as concrete, which can be given an interesting finish (*see pp.44–45*) to prevent gray "runways" crossing the garden. If gravel is your preferred choice, use a grade that is large enough not to wedge in the bottoms of your shoes but small enough to allow you to walk on it comfortably (*see p.49*).

Where paths will be used frequently – especially by children – try to plan along usage lines. These lines usually run along the shortest distance between two points; if the path is on an inconvenient route, it will not be taken. Curved corners on a

DIRECTLY TO YOUR DOOR

In some situations, the most appropriate route between A and B is a straight line. This short, front path is wide and straight enough to permit easy passage, especially when burdened with shopping, strollers, or other domestic paraphernalia. This harmonious layout illustrates how even the strictly functional can be made attractive. Its style and colors match both the period of the house and the materials used in its construction.

▲ ACCESS TO A BORDER
A series of stepping-stones provides practical access across a planting. It allows plants to be tended and protects hidden bulbs or dormant plants from being stepped on.

◀ A MEANDERING PATH
The sinuous curves of this path invite exploration by suggesting that there are hidden features just around the next corner.

path will prevent shortcuts from being taken across right angled bends, which usually result in worn lawns or compacted soil in borders. Curves are much easier to negotiate with a wheelbarrow or mower.

Paths do not always need to be paved or graveled. Small paths of stepping-stones provide useful access through borders to tend the plants. Grass paths at the back of deep borders are handy for occasional access when a hedge needs trimming.

LEADING THE EYE

One of the main design functions to consider when laying a path is how it will draw the eye from one area to another. A straight path tends to reveal all, but if a focal feature concludes the vista, it pleases the eye. This need not mean that all of the garden is seen at once – site other paths so that they are discovered only as the main path is traversed. For most people, a curved path, which seldom reveals the garden in one sweep, is too tempting to

> For most people, a curved path is just too tempting to leave unexplored

leave unexplored. A seat at the crossroads of paths will allow enjoyment of several views from a single point, but it can lack a sense of privacy. A resting place in a niche at the end of a path makes a secluded spot from which to contemplate the plants as well as enjoy a view.

MORE PRACTICAL CONSIDERATIONS

IT IS VITALLY IMPORTANT TO CONSIDER the width of your proposed paths since it is all too easy to make them too narrow. Where surrounding planting is tall or overhanging, even an otherwise roomy path seems narrow and, in wet weather, will be impossible to traverse without getting a soaking as you brush past. Low, creeping plants – even when they are used to soften hard edges – can also encroach on the width, and usefulness, of an access path.

PRACTICAL CONSIDERATIONS

Twists and turns in paths and steps lend character to a garden but are no fun if you are wheeling compost along them. Take time choosing routes and identifying their primary purpose. The formal style of a parterre, for example, positively demands narrow paths set at right angles to each other to enclose small beds, but this style of garden seldom calls for heavy wheelbarrow work. If access for garden equipment is needed regularly, wide paths with rounded corners will be more appropriate. Curves should be broad and sweeping rather than tight and wiggling – generous curves are easier to negotiate as well as to construct. If changes in level are to be negotiated using steps, consider the height of risers and width of tread. Broad, shallow steps allow easy passage with equipment; deeper steps are suited only to foot traffic.

▲ ADDING LIGHT
Adequate and attractive lighting not only renders these steps safe in the dark, it brings an added dimension to the design at night.

▼ FOCAL POINT
Generous paths add to the impact of a garden feature, while small pavers make a safe surface and are easily laid in a circular design.

SUNKEN GARDEN
This sunken garden is an attractive feature but is less than ideal for a family garden used by small children or infirm adults. The change in level would be safer to negotiate had a shallow stepped entrance been incorporated into the feature. Lighting would improve safety at night.

SAFE AND EASY ACCESS

The surfaces of main paths must be kept clear of clutter if they are not to prove a potential cause of accidents. Taking this into account, make them wide enough so they can be lined with plants, pots, or other ornaments, thus combining use with beauty. Ample width is especially important

> ### Keep paths that are in frequent use free of hazardous clutter

where paths meet to form a crossroads, particularly if you wish to use the opportunity to create a focal point shared by all the paths.

Where paths take unexpected turns, or if steps must be used regularly in the dark, it is worth installing lighting; lights confer safety and security and also bring life and atmosphere to the garden at night.

The surface of paths and steps is also a vital safety consideration. While textural variation often plays an important role in a design, it is best restricted to margins or other areas of light traffic. Level, even, and nonslip surfaces are essential for safe access, especially if they are to be used by the very young, very old, or infirm.

PLANNING PATHS

- Make paths wide enough to allow easy access; allow 5ft/1.5m for free access along practical paths for gardening tasks or for people to walk side by side.
- Keep path networks simple.
- Make sure paving surfaces are nonslip, level, and even. Keep textural changes level with adjacent surfaces. Restrict any raised textural detail to areas of low traffic.
- Make changes in level obvious to avoid the chance of tripping.
- Step edges can be highlighted with a paler material, and use lighting at night for extra safety and security.

DECORATIVE SURFACES

Paving serves more than a practical purpose – if materials are carefully chosen, it can be beautiful to look at, can link house and outdoors, and provide a perfect foil for plantings. But with such a wealth of materials available, there is always a temptation to use too many, resulting in a busy and distracting effect. The most pleasing results will be gained with a restricted range of materials, selected to tie in with the style and color of the house and other garden features.

UNITY AND VARIETY

The overriding principle designers use when choosing decorative materials is to strike a balance between unity and variety. Although it is easy to unite a single material with the other materials used in a garden, a large expanse is likely to look monotonous and will need a little variety to bring it to life.

Large areas of slabs can be broken up by interspersing them, for example, with lines of bricks or terracotta tiles laid on edge. Gravel and stones laid in concrete can also break up stark areas of paving. You can use contrasts in color or texture to mark out main routes or delineate areas for seating or dining. Changes of level can be incorporated into a paving plan and will add visual appeal, especially in the form of steps or raised beds.

In large expanses of paving, you can make spaces for planting by leaving out occasional slabs or, alternatively, avoid monotony by placing attractive pots and barrels of plants on the paved surface.

MIXING MATERIALS
Wooden decking with color-matched gravel (above) ties in with a path with a wooden raised bed. A large area of paving (right) is relieved by an elegant contrast of color and texture created by setting in a panel of water-worn pebbles.

STYLIZED PAVING
Here, a simple gravel surface blends perfectly with the dominant feature, while subtle color and textural contrast is provided by stepping-stones. The stone lantern has inspired a thoughtful selection of a limited range of materials, which have then been used to create an appropriate Oriental-style setting.

USING TEXTURE AND COLOR

When choosing colors and textures, take note of – and try to blend with – those used in the house and other features. In country gardens, you may also wish to consider the surrounding landscape. The synthetic tints of brightly colored paving look unnatural in rural areas and seldom

> Brightly colored materials can work well in urban gardens

blend well with materials used in older properties. Here, recycled materials with an aged appearance may look best. But in modern urban gardens, bright colors combine well with painted walls, stylish ceramics, or furniture. In general, though, more subtle textural contrasts, using the natural palette of warm browns, cool grays, and terracotta, are easiest to place.

Wood is particularly versatile: it can be stained in natural or bright colors and, in itself, provides a variety of textures, from rough-hewn to smooth and planed. Use color and textural contrasts to define path or patio edges, to enliven large areas of paving, or simply to add interest to areas designated for seating.

CHOOSING MATERIALS

In most cases, good results are achieved by using materials that already exist on your property. The color and fabric of the house will probably be the main influence on your choice of paving material. For a brick house, for example, paving edged with or made from brick or terracotta tiles would suit. Similarly, aged brick and mellow wood complement the honey tones of sandstone.

If your area is to include wooden features such as a summerhouse or pergola, wooden decking may be an appropriate choice.

A rock garden may dictate the color of a nearby stone path – materials from the same local source will usually blend perfectly.

MIMICKING NATURE

Creators of gardens have long sought inspiration from the natural world and, for many gardeners, natural effects are still the most prized. A path that mimics a dried-up river bed, studded with colonizing plants, is

---

Display maritime plants next to a path of sea-washed pebbles

---

not only a route through the garden but an opportunity to grow a greater diversity of plants. Crushed slate or gravel resembles a mountain scree and makes an ideal home for alpine plants, while sea-washed pebbles make a perfect foil for maritime plants, such as sea lavender or thrift. In coastal gardens, crushed shells make a good, crunchy path if laid like gravel.

Wood is a natural choice for a woodland setting, and slabs of tree trunk, set among bark chips, look perfectly appropriate. Railroad ties are ideal for constructing long-lasting paths and are very effective if set in bark or gravel and interplanted with species native to the woodland floor.

ABSTRACT DESIGN

Small, modern plots lend themselves well to experiments with abstract designs; here, you might seek inspiration from the works of modern artists. A geometric hard-edged layout of different materials can form a

▲ RECLAIMED MATERIALS
Old railroad ties, which are impregnated with creosote, make a long-lasting material for imaginative paths. As with other reclaimed materials, they come ready-aged and mellow.

▶ A RIVER OF SLATE
Japanese and Chinese garden-makers take inspiration from, and echo, the natural world. Here, a ribbon of crushed slate suggests a babbling brook in contrast to the limpid water contained within the tsukubai, *a traditional ornamental bowl.*

framework for plants to create a living patchwork of color. Here, caution can be thrown to the wind; mundane paving can be set beside materials of bright color with the spaces between filled with plants and gravel. Areas of the patchwork can be made into smaller individual compositions, with planting that coordinates with the paving materials. A checkered pattern of slabs and soil is a popular way to grow

CHECKERED COURSE
An abstract design divided into small units can eke out expensive decorative materials to cover a relatively large area.

elaborate designs. And do not underestimate the value of reclaimed, recycled, or found objects, for their use can often put a highly individual mark on your designs. Wood, whether new or reclaimed, can be painted or stained to add an extra dimension and interesting textures in the garden.

Throw caution to the wind and offset mundane paving with bright color

---

herbs, alpines, and bulbs, allowing the plants to grow through gravel or chips. Dividing up an area into smaller units often means that you can eke out relatively costly materials over a fairly large area without breaking the bank. In small areas, you can be as creative as you like: expensive materials such as glass beads or polished pebbles can be placed alongside contrasting evergreen plants, or broken ceramic tiles can be used to create picture mosaics or

INSPIRATION

• Visit friends' gardens and those open to the public armed with a notebook. Jot down any exciting uses of materials that catch your eye. Modify them to make them your own.

• Supply stores and salvage yards may get you buzzing with ideas, and don't overlook plumbing items – utilitarian copper pieces acquire an attractive verdigris with age.

• Magazines and books on gardening are rich sources of visual stimulation, but so too are those concerned with interior design.

• Look to nature: the seashore, the forest floor, mountain screes, and water margins all hold inspiration for the observant gardener.

FINISHING TOUCHES

THE EDGING AND PLANTS AROUND a path can greatly enhance its appearance. Edging prevents loose material from spreading into flower beds; low, creeping plants disguise harsh edges and bring a natural look to new paths. To help increase the impression of width, keep plants that overhang main paths to no higher than shoulder height. To accentuate a formal look, choose a low plant, such as lavender or *Santolina*, and grow it along both sides or at regular intervals.

ADDING PLANTS

In sunny parts of the garden, fragrant plants such as herbs, gray-leaved pinks, and lavender are a good choice for path edges and will release their fragrance as you brush past them. Creeping plants such as thymes and chamomile can be put into gaps between slabs or grown through gravel, but avoid putting clumps in the way of the main access paths where they may not survive treading and might cause an accident. They are ideal beneath seats where they can be enjoyed at leisure, and their fragrance will heighten your sense of relaxation. Put pots and containers of temporary and permanent plants at the

COOL CONTRAST
The color warmth of the hard materials used in this design draws the eye and lifts the beauty of this cool-color border to higher levels. Scented plants release fragrance as they are brushed against providing another, more ethereal dimension.
The height gained by the judicious siting of a planted terracotta urn – blending seamlessly with warm brick paving – reflects and echoes the rising steps that terminate the vista.

edges of paving to help the hard surface blend into the surrounding planting, or in groups to break up the effect of large areas.

SOFT EDGING

Neat plants make a good edging for paths. Among the most popular is dwarf boxwood, which can be clipped to keep it

> Hostas are excellent edging plants, with a wide variety of leaf sizes

to just 6in/15cm. Lavender and *Santolina* can also be clipped as a formal low hedge. A formal look can be enhanced by the symmetrical planting of architectural plants, such as yuccas, at intervals along the length of a path. London pride (*Saxifraga* × *urbium*), *Bergenia*, and pinks make low cushions of foliage and are evergreen. Hostas are excellent edging plants: with their wide variation in leaf size they can match, or contrast with, the surface. Brick paving accentuates the size of large-leaved varieties; smaller-leaved hostas are in scale with narrow paths. Although hostas are deciduous, they can be underplanted with spring-flowering bulbs, and the hostas will disguise their yellowing foliage.

▲ INFORMAL EDGING
Neat, rosette-forming alpines, such as this Sempervivum, *quickly colonize well-drained planting pockets between paving.*

▼ FORMAL EDGING
The precise line of these period edging tiles accentuates the neat, crisp finish of this immaculately clipped dwarf boxwood hedge.

PLANTS FOR PAVED AREAS

FOR PLANTING POCKETS			FOR FRAGRANCE
Acaena microphylla	*Hebe* (many)	*Rhodanthemum*	*Artemisia caucasica*
Ajuga reptans	*Helianthemum* (many)	*Salvia officinalis*	A. schmidtiana
Alchemilla (most)	*Jovibarba* (many)	*Saponaria ocymoides*	A. stelleriana
Armeria maritima	*Lamium maculatum*	*Saxifraga* × *urbium*	*Chamaemelum nobile*
Aubrieta (many)	*Ophiopogon planiscapus*	*Sedum* (many)	'Treneague' *
Ceratostigma	*Persicaria affinis*	*Sempervivum* (most)	*Mentha pulegium*
Erinus alpinus	*Phlox subulata*	*Sisyrinchium striatum*	M. requienii*
Euphorbia cyparissias	*Plantago nivalis*	*Stachys byzantina*	*Salvia officinalis*
E. myrsinites	*Potentilla alba*	*Viola riviniana* Purpurea Group	*Thymus serpyllum* *
Festuca glauca	*Pratia* (most)	*Yucca filamentosa*	
	Raoulia australis		* withstands treading

HARD EDGING

A neat, permanent edging is the perfect way to finish a path. It is aesthetically pleasing and, by retaining border soil and preventing the path from becoming messy, it is also practical. Modern reproductions of traditional Victorian terracotta rope tiles, while expensive, are durable and suit both formal and informal designs.

Reclaimed materials can be both practical and inexpensive

Concrete curbing is cheap and appropriate in modern settings, but for more elegant effects, there are prettier alternatives such as cast stone edging. Reclaimed materials such as roof tiles and wood are both practical and inexpensive and, with imagination, can make unusual edges to paths.

PATIO DECORATION

A diverse range of pots, barrels and urns is available to provide decoration for patios. Filled with tender plants, they can lend the illusion of tropical warmth during the summer months, while spring bedding provides color early in the year. A garden

LAWN MEETS PAVING
A hard edge is softened as grass penetrates the cracks between the pavers. Make sure pavers are lower than the grass for easy mowing.

ornament set among them, or isolated to emphasize its presence, will complete the effect. But whether you use a group of pots or ornaments, or a single large one as a focal point, for safety's sake, do not place them on busy corners and keep them to the edges on steps and main routes. If used with discretion and grouped with regard to their size and height, they elevate a design without creating clutter.

FORMAL EDGING
Modern, molded clay edging tiles are frost-resistant and make a neat and durable edge for formal borders.

SEASHELL EDGING
Seashells introduce a whimsical element to edging, but avoid those with a sharp edge in gardens where children have access.

LAYING PATHS AND SURFACES

THE FOLLOWING PAGES cover a selection of simple projects using a range of materials and techniques that gardeners with few building skills – or none at all – can tackle safely and confidently to produce satisfying results in usually no more than a weekend. Bear in mind

RIGID PAVING

that the durability of all surfaces depends on the use of construction methods appropriate to each type of material, and that the true cost includes not only initial outlay but also the degree of maintenance required and the expected lifespan. Rigid paving (*see p.25*) made from precast slabs – available in a wealth of shapes, sizes, and colors – is one of the most expensive, but provided that slabs are securely laid onto a properly prepared base, they last for many decades. Flexible paving (*see p.35*), made from

FLEXIBLE PAVING

cobblestones, setts, or bricks bedded on sand, is also expensive but hard-wearing. It may lift or sag in places with age and need a little attention. Gravel (*see p.49*), although one of the most attractive and least costly of materials, may need replenishing regularly and demands frequent attention to weed control. Although relatively cheap, durable, and easy to lay, concrete (*see p.41*) has a utilitarian image that

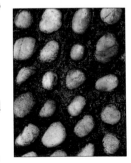

DECORATIVE CONCRETE

belies its versatility in the creation of decorative surfaces. Wooden decking (*see p.57*) is extremely stylish and moderately expensive. It is simple to construct and, if treated with suitable

WOODEN DECKING

preservatives, has an expected life of 25 years or more.

FORMAL PAVING

To MAKE FORMAL, smooth, permanent paving bedded onto and jointed with mortar, and to add clearly defined, well-built steps and low walls, you need to use professional construction methods and to pay strict attention to levels and measurements, because an unsatisfactory result will be hard to remedy. A firm foundation is crucial, because if it moves, slabs may crack. Provided that the project is not too ambitious, the building skills involved are not hard to master.

LAYING PERMANENT PAVING

The laying of any permanent surface should be carefully thought through before you even visit a builders' supplier. Deciding the location, shape, and materials to be used and how best to lay them depends on factors such as how much use or traffic the surface will receive, the relative size of the area, and the materials used in existing buildings and structures.

The essence of the formal style lies in crisp geometry and balanced symmetry, which is, in practical terms, most easily achieved by laying slabs of uniform size and shape, as here, on firm foundations. You can relax the style to include softer lines and curves by using variably sized materials such as random paving, small, warm-toned units such as bricks laid in patterns and spirals, or pavers that are specially shaped to produce circular designs.

BEFORE YOU START

- Before undertaking any excavation work, locate underground utilities, such as water or gas pipes and electricity, television, or telephone cables, to avoid damaging them. You must leave meters and covers unobstructed.
- Any surface that butts up directly to a house wall should have some sort of divider between it and the wall and incorporate a slight drainage slope (*see next page*) that sheds water away from the house foundations.
- You should not walk on the paving, once laid, for 24 hours, or ideally two days. Do not pave yourself into a corner, and think about how you will keep traffic off the area.

FOUNDATION
FOR PAVING
*The key to success
with paving is in the
preparation of a firm
and level base, built
up from several layers
of materials.*

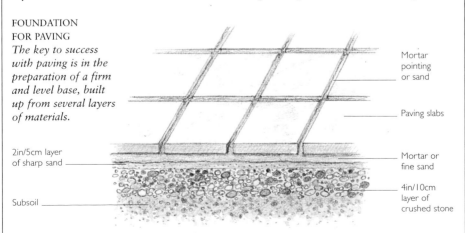

Mortar
pointing
or sand

Paving slabs

2in/5cm layer
of sharp sand

Mortar or
fine sand

4in/10cm
layer of
crushed stone

Subsoil

◄ OFFSET SLABS *Cutting some slabs allows unobtrusive patterning instead of a rigid checkerboard.*

YOU NEED:

MATERIALS
- Crushed stone to cover area to compacted depth of 4in/10cm
- Sharp sand to cover crushed stone to depth of 2in/5cm
- Slabs (allow an extra 5% of total quantity for breakage if you need to cut to size)
- Mortar mix
- Edging of choice (see p.28)

TOOLS
- Marking pegs
- String
- Framing square
- Spade
- Level
- Mason's chisel
- Maul
- Wood board
- Masonry trowel
- Spacers (½in/1cm dowel cut into 2in/5cm lengths)
- Brush

TOOL RENTAL
- Power compactor

LAYING THE FOUNDATIONS

1 **Use pegs and string** to mark out the area to be paved. Check that the corners are at right angles using a framing square.

2 **Dig down** to firm subsoil; allow 6in/15cm for stone and sand plus the depth of the surface layer. Tamp with power compactor.

3 **Insert marking pegs** in a grid at 6½ft/2m intervals as level guides. Incorporate a slight fall (see drainage slope, below) to allow surface water to drain away. Use a level to ensure pegs and string are level.

4 **Add a layer** of stone; compact to 4in/10cm; check levels. Add a layer of sand and compact to 2in/5cm.

DRAINAGE SLOPE

A paved surface should slope with a slight fall of approximately 1in/2.5cm per 6½ft/2m to permit surface drainage of water. First mark a number of pegs, at the same distance from the top end of each. Drive the pegs in, in rows about 6½ft/2m apart – the first row of pegs at the top of the slope with the marks at soil level. In the second row, put a 1in/2.5cm scrap on each peg. Lay a level on a board between this peg and one in the first row. Adjust the height of the lower peg so the top of the scrap and the upper peg are level. Remove the scrap. Repeat down the slope.

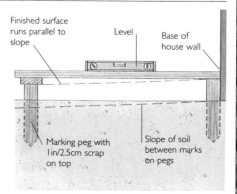

Finished surface runs parallel to slope

Level

Base of house wall

Marking peg with 1in/2.5cm scrap on top

Slope of soil between marks on pegs

CUTTING PAVING SLABS TO FIT

1 **On a flat,** firm surface, use a mason's chisel blade to score a groove on both faces and edges of the slab.

2 **Work along** the scored line with a mason's chisel and maul to deepen the groove on the slab.

3 **Place the slab** on a length of wood. Align the groove with the wood edge; tap the slab with a maul until it splits.

LAYING THE PAVING SLABS

1 **Start laying the slabs** at the house wall or other defined edge. Spread strips of mortar in a square just smaller than the slab. Add a cross strip for large slabs.

2 **Position the slab** on the mortar and tap it down. Use a level to check that it is level. Repeat over the area, using spacers to create ½in/1cm gaps between the slabs.

3 **Take out the spacers** before the mortar sets. After 2 days or so, fill in between the slabs with sand or bedding mortar. You might want to use a jigger (*inset*). Aligning the central slit of this device with the small gap between 2 slabs allows the gap to be filled without the risk of spilling onto the slabs. Tamp down the material so it is just barely recessed. Brush the slabs clean.

FINISHING PATIOS AND PAVING

Once the slabs have been laid, the surface may be finished with edging. Edging serves a number of purposes, some practical, others decorative. Most immediately, it defines an area, separating it from adjacent lawns and flower beds. On a more practical level, when a surface is made up using flexible material, edging holds that material in place and confines it within the desired area. You can use the same material for edging or introduce another surface to contrast with and complement the principal paving. In terms of style, the more decorative the edging, the less formal the finish. Possible materials include wood, brick, pavers and tiles. If using wood, make sure that it has been pressure-treated with preservative. Bricks, tiles, or pavers may be mortared in so that there is no chance of them shifting on the base.

PAVERS AS EDGING
Pavers create a neat finish to a patio's edge. The diagram (right) *shows how simple they are to put in place. When set below the level of an adjacent lawn, they permit easy mowing.*

MIXED-MATERIAL EDGING
Here, a mixture of treated log sections and pavers is set in concrete to produce an attractive edge to a patio. A raised edge keeps plants and loose mulches within bounds.

PAVERS AS EDGING

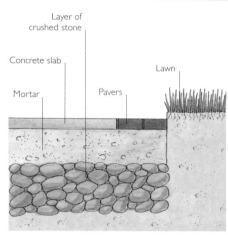

Layer of crushed stone

Concrete slab

Mortar

Pavers

Lawn

MIXED MATERIAL EDGING

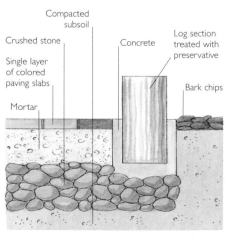

Compacted subsoil

Crushed stone

Single layer of colored paving slabs

Mortar

Concrete

Log section treated with preservative

Bark chips

ALTERNATIVE FORMAL SURFACES

A variety of materials such as random paving, setts, and bricks, whether found, reclaimed, or purchased, can be used for formal surfaces. They must be capable of providing an even, nonslip surface for walking and be sufficiently robust to withstand severe weather conditions. Their strength should match the load that they need to bear – whether it is foot or vehicular traffic, for example.

BRICK PAVING
Bricks make an even and attractive hard surface. If using reclaimed bricks, make sure that they are weatherproof; building bricks, used for facing houses, for example, tend to flake if subjected to a freeze-thaw cycle.

PREFORMED PAVING SLABS

Garden centers stock a variety of preformed paving slabs, which can be fitted together to form a complete surface. Flexible units in circular, octagonal, and interlocking shapes come in a range of materials and colors. Some units look like several fitted together. They are quickly and easily laid to create complex and finely textured effects. Keyed blocks or slabs are specially designed for the construction of curves and circles without complex cutting.

KEYED SLABS

MOLDED CEMENT SLAB

BRICK-EFFECT SLAB

HEXAGONAL TERRACOTTA TILE BLOCK

LAYING RANDOM PAVING

To make a really smooth, safe surface out of random paving, it is best to lay it on stone or sand, with bedding mortar filling the gaps for a more impervious surface. When laying the paving, position edging material first, and secure it in place with mortar so that the boundaries are clearly defined or, as below, cut a straight edge in grass to butt the paving up against it. Working from one corner of the area, first dry-lay an area of about 3ft/1m square without mortar, fitting the pieces together like a puzzle. Keep the gaps small. Once satisfied with their placement, fill with sand or bedding mortar. Check that they are level with the edge pieces using a straightedge and level, before moving on to fill the rest of the area.

A UNIQUE FINISH
Here, dappled sunshine on random paving adds a lovely touch to the garden. The beauty of this paving is that each surface is unique.

1 **Using string lines** and pegs to mark the height of the edges, lay foundations (*see p.26*). Then lay the edging pieces, placing their straight edges outermost.

2 **Fill the center** with large slabs, and fill in with small ones. Using wood and a maul, bed them on the foundation. Keep the central slabs level with the edging pieces.

3 **Fill the cracks** with crumbly, almost dry mortar, or brush in sand. If using a dark-colored stone such as slate, a concrete dye will make the cracks less conspicuous.

4 **If applying a mortar finish,** use a pointing trowel to bevel the mortar so that any surface water drains quickly away from the slabs.

LAYING BRICKS

Using bricks to construct a patio is a great way of visually linking a brick house with the yard. Bricks are more versatile as paving than stone or concrete slabs, since they can be laid in a variety of patterns.

Given the wide range of bricks available, it should be easy to find a type that suits you. Contact local builders' supply stores for large quantities, and make sure that the bricks are frost-resistant.

1 **Prepare foundations** (*see p.26*), allowing space for edging bricks. For small areas, the subbase can be tamped with a piece of wood rather than a power compactor.

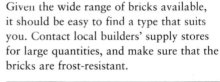
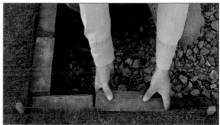

2 Use **string lines and pegs** to set edging bricks at desired height. If edges butt up to a lawn, make the finished level of edging just below the lawn surface for ease of mowing.

3 **Lay the edging bricks** on a concrete footing, then mortar the cracks. Lay the rest onto the foundation and tamp them level. At intervals, check the levels in all directions.

4 **Spread a thin layer** of dry mortar or sand over the brickwork surface, then brush it between the cracks. Sprinkle with water (*inset*) to set the mortar, then clean the surface.

LAYING BRICKS IN PATTERNS

Bricks may be laid in several simple ways to create attractive patterns, such as those shown here; the herringbone pattern requires bricks to be cut to fit at the margins of the area. In areas with little frost penetration of the soil, bricks can be laid on a 1in/2.5cm layer of bedding mortar. Dry mortar used for pointing is self-setting in wet weather, but setting time can be speeded up by sprinkling with water. In colder areas, lay bricks on a well-prepared foundation and sand bed (*see p.35*). Use thin strips of wood as spacers, if desired.

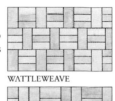

WATTLEWEAVE

PARQUET/BASKETWEAVE

HALF BASKETWEAVE

HERRINGBONE

CHANGING LEVELS

There are a number of ways to change a flat, featureless area into one that incorporates different levels. Low walls, steps, and raised beds are all features that can eliminate the visual boredom of a single level. They add visual interest and can have practical benefits. A low wall, for example, can offer protection to plants from wind and cold. Steps cut into a slope draw the eye into an area where previously there may only have been a bland grassy incline and make access across the area much easier. Use the same, or complementary, materials as the patio for a unifying effect (*see facing page*).

BUILDING A LOW WALL

A low wall, whether used to execute a change in level or to create a raised bed, is a simple project. If less than a yard/meter in height, it requires few technical skills and – although it is always wise to check – is unlikely to violate any local building ordinances. When siting a low wall, consider whether it is to act as a barrier or you need to gain safe access across it. You may need to build in a step for any wall higher than 8–10in/20–25cm, the maximum comfortable distance to step down safely without risk of stumbling.

A DEFINING WALL
This low wall of reconstituted stone blocks is quite easy to build and gives the raised lawn a neat and strongly defined boundary.

WALL FOUNDATIONS

A low wall must be built on a solid foundation such as concrete blocks; these are bedded into the stone base of the adjacent paving so that the edges of the blocks align with the edges of the paving. Build the wall so that the first brick will be level with the paving, then insert small-diameter pipes to form drainage weepholes (*right*), or leave vertical cracks between bricks on the next layer unfilled with mortar. Lay the paving so that the mortar extends over the edge of the concrete blocks to lock them in place and leave a 2in/5cm gap between paving and wall. Fill the gap, and that between the wall and soil, with coarse gravel to stop the weepholes from becoming clogged.

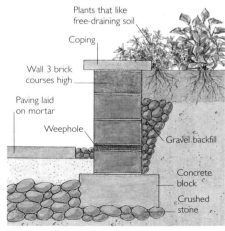

Plants that like free-draining soil

Coping

Wall 3 brick courses high

Paving laid on mortar

Weephole

Gravel backfill

Concrete block

Crushed stone

CONSTRUCTING SIMPLE STEPS

Calculate the number of steps you need by dividing the height of the slope by the total height of one riser (including slab and mortar). To measure slope height, place a peg at the top of the slope and a post at the bottom. Tie string between the two so it is level with the top of the slope; measure the distance between the string and ground level.

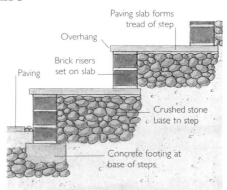

STEPPING SAFELY

Treads should be at least 12in/30cm deep from front to back, with a maximum 2in/5cm overhang and risers 4–7in/10–18cm high.

SIMPLE STEPS WITH PAVING SLABS

1 Use **string and pegs** to mark the sides of the steps, then run strings along the fronts of the treads. Dig out the steps and compact the soil for each tread area.

2 **Make a footing** 6in/15cm deep and twice the brick width; fill with concrete over a 3in/8cm stone base. Lay first riser on the set concrete footing; check the bricks are level.

3 **Fill risers with stone** to the height of the bricks and tamp down. Set the slabs on ½in/1cm of mortar, with an overhang of 1–2in/2.5–5cm at the front. Leave a small gap.

4 **Mark the position** of the second riser on the slabs; mortar the bricks in place. Fill in and set the treads as before. Continue with the remaining steps. Mortar between the slabs.

The following labels appear in the illustration:

Paving slab forms tread of step

Overhang

Brick risers set on slab

Paving

Crushed stone base to step

Concrete footing at base of steps

INFORMAL PAVING

WHEN YOU LAY OUT AN AREA in an informal style, you have free rein in the choice of materials for paving and other surfaces and for textural detail and color combinations that would be out of place in formal gardens. However, the materials must still be practical and safe. Informal designs lend themselves to flexible paving, bedded in sand and kept in place with a fixed edge. It is easy to lay and to replace single units and is more forgiving of mistakes.

MAKING AN INFORMAL PAVED AREA

A surface constructed from materials of varying shapes and sizes has integral textural variety that lends charm and interest of itself. Often, the most successful results are to be had by combining materials that share a common range of color tone. Bear in mind the danger of creating busy and jumbled effects by using too many different elements of color and texture.

FOR THE BEST RESULTS

• Ensure that walking surfaces are even and nonslip, keeping less regular, high-definition textures to the margins of an area.

• When using irregularly shaped units of different depths, adjust the depth at which each unit is bedded to create level surfaces.

• Use the aged, mellow appearance of reclaimed materials to introduce informality seamlessly into established areas at relatively low cost.

ESSENTIAL CALCULATIONS
Do your math first, especially if using found or reclaimed materials. Calculate roughly the size of each area to be filled with each different material so that you don't run out before the design is finished.

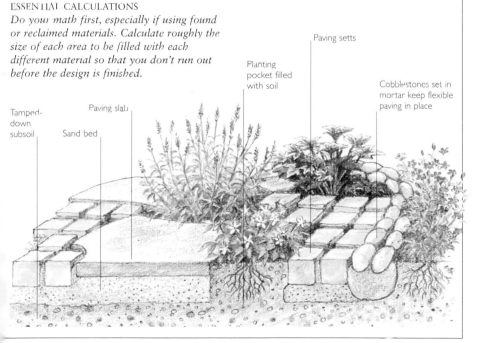

Paving setts

Planting
pocket filled
with soil

Cobblestones set in
mortar keep flexible
paving in place

Tamped-
down
subsoil

Paving slab

Sand bed

INFORMAL CURVES *A sinuous edging of cobblestones borders loosely laid setts.*

YOU NEED:

MATERIALS
- Paving materials: paving slabs and granite setts
- Sharp sand for a 3in/8cm covering of base area
- Cobblestones to edge
- Mortar mix to bed cobblestones

TOOLS
- Spade
- Wooden post
- Rake
- Trowel
- Level
- Maul
- Brush • Bucket

PREPARING THE BASE

1 **Mark out** the area, then dig it out to form a level base of compacted soil. Make it deep enough to hold a 2in/5cm layer of firmed sand plus the thickness of the slabs so that the paved area will be level with surrounding beds. Small areas such as this can be tamped firm using a wooden post (*see p.31*). Use a power compactor for larger areas.

2 **Add a layer** of sharp sand to cover the entire area; a depth of about 3in/8cm will firm down to 2in/5cm.

3 **Rake the sand** smooth and level by eye, paying attention to filling any voids or irregularities at the edges.

4 **Firm the sand** to create a bedding layer. Tread down with your feet to give a final depth of about 2in/5cm.

MAKING THE FIXED EDGE

1 **Arrange the cobblestones** and, when satisfied, mortar in place. Settle them into the mortar a few at a time to form a level edge that is higher than surrounding beds.

2 **Place the largest pieces** of paving into position first on the sand bed. Add or subtract sand below each slab until they are all sitting level with each other.

3 **Check the level** of the slabs one with another using a level. Tamp down with the handle of a maul. The slabs should also be level with surrounding beds.

4 **Lay the setts** approximately level with the slabs, adjusting height as necessary by scooping out more or less sand. Fit them fairly closely to prevent them from moving.

5 **When the setts** are in place and settled securely into the sand, finish bedding them in by tamping them down firmly with the handle of a maul.

6 **Using a level,** check that the setts are level with the slabs as you go. Remember to leave some small areas unpaved to act as pockets for planting.

FINISHING THE PAVING

1 **Add a final layer** of dry, sharp sand mixed with a little fine soil, using a trowel. Add enough sand and soil mix to cover the setts, slabs, and any small gaps between them.

2 **Using a soft brush,** sweep the sand and soil mix into the gaps between setts and slabs. Remove any air pockets by firming the sand with a narrow piece of wood.

PLANTING THE POCKETS

1 **To make a planting hole,** first remove as much sand and soil mix as possible from the planting pocket. Scoop it into a bucket to keep the paving free of soil, then discard it.

2 **Fill in the planting hole** with a mixture of good soil and well-rotted organic matter. Use a trowel to work the mixture well into the surrounding soil.

3 **Dig a hole for each plant,** deep and wide enough to accommodate the rootball. Insert plant, backfill with soil mix, and firm to eliminate any air pockets around the roots.

4 **Sweep any spilled soil mix** into the planting pocket before watering the plant well. This avoids creating muddy patches. The area is then top-dressed (*see facing page*).

PLANTING IN CREVICES

To sow seed (right), brush away any top-dressing, if necessary; trickle in soil mix. Sow seed thinly, cover with a thin layer of coarse sand, and water in. Small plug plants establish rapidly. Make a planting hole and insert the plant. Back-fill with soil mix. Firm and water in.

SOWING SEED

USING PLUG PLANTS

TOP-DRESSING THE PLANTED AREA

When you have completed planting, top-dress all soil surfaces with a layer of coarse sand, grit, or fine-grade gravel. This adds a unifying element to the design and acts as a mulch, excluding light and helping to prevent the germination of weed seeds. Also, it will help keep plant roots cool and moist in summer. A grit top-dressing around the necks of vulnerable plants, such as alpines and silver-leaved plants, provides excellent drainage and reduces the risk of fatal damage in cold, wet winters.

KEEPING UP APPEARANCES
Keep the plants well watered while they are becoming established. Thereafter, they need little additional water except during prolonged periods of dry weather. Keep the area free of weeds by hand-weeding or by spot-weeding with a suitable herbicide, following the manufacturer's instructions.

GOOD PLANTS FOR PAVING

PLANTS FOR POCKETS

Achillea clypeolata
Aethionema (most)
Alchemilla alpina, A. conjuncta
Anthemis punctata subsp. *cupaniana*
Arabis caucasica
Armeria maritima
Artemisia schmidtiana 'Nana'
Buxus microphylla 'Green Pillow'
Campanula arvatica, C. carpatica
Dianthus alpinus, D. arenarius
Euphorbia polychroma
Geranium dalmaticum, G. clarkei
Hebe cupressoides 'Boughton Dome'
Helichrysum italicum
Heuchera micrantha 'Palace Purple'

Heuchera 'Pewter Moon'
Iberis (most)
Lavandula angustifolia 'Munstead'
Potentilla alba
Veronica prostrata 'Trehane'
Viola 'Huntercombe Purple', V. 'Jackanapes'

PLANTS FOR CREVICES

Arenaria balearica, A. montana
Campanula cochleariifolia
Chamaemelum nobile 'Treneague'
Leptinella atrata
Mentha requienii
Sempervivum (most)
Soleirolia soleirolii
Thymus pseudolanuginosus, T. serpyllum

CONCRETES AND MORTARS

CONCRETE IS A FAR MORE VERSATILE surface than its drab image suggests. Apart from the fact that it is relatively quick and easy to lay, it can be painted and textured to create a totally new surface while retaining the qualities of durability and resilience. It is also an excellent matrix in which to set materials such as cobblestones and other decorative aggregates.

LAYING CONCRETE

A plain stretch of concrete (*see next page*) may be just what you need – for a driveway, perhaps – but you can also use concrete and mortar mixes as bases in which to create interesting textures. Use a stiff-bristled broom to add contrast by exposing aggregate (*p.44*), or insert pebbles (*p.45*), cobblestones, or glass nuggets to create mosaic effects. Alternatively, leaves, seashells, and other natural forms make stamped patterns (*p.46*) in concrete.

WORKING WITH CEMENT

- If the site is large, divide it into smaller sections no bigger than 13ft/4m long.
- If mixing your own concrete, start by adding one part water to two parts cement, and then gradually add more water.
- If the mixture gets too wet, sprinkle in a small amount of dry cement and quickly work it in, making sure that no lumps form.
- Avoid laying concrete if the temperature is close to freezing or over 90°F/32°C.
- Store bags of cement on raised boards, and cover them with a plastic sheet to keep dry.

PEBBLE INLAY
Making a feature of mortar pointing between slabs – by studding it with pebbles, for example – adds variety and makes expensive paving materials go further.

◄ PATTERNED FINISH *Glazed ceramic balls set in concrete can produce a stylish surface.*

YOU NEED:

MATERIALS
- 8 1in/3cm wooden form boards
- 2in/5cm nails
- Crushed stone to cover base area to 4in/10cm
- Concrete to cover stone to 4in/10cm
- Plastic sheeting

TOOLS
- Pegs, string
- Screed board
- Framing square
- Spade • Level
- Hammer
- Maul
- Roller
- Wooden beam
- Masonry trowel
- Float

For areas over 40 sq.ft/4 sq.m, renting a concrete mixer is advisable; they are usually available by the day.

MAKING A WOODEN FRAMEWORK

1 **Having marked out** the site (see p.26, step 1), dig it out to a depth of 8in/20cm and drive leveling pegs into the ground 3ft/1m apart along string lines. Align them horizontally using a screed board and a level.

2 **Remove** the string lines and nail boards to the inner faces of the pegs, butted end to end at the corners. Use a maul to hold the plank steady. This framework holds the concrete in place until it sets hard.

ADDING A CRUSHED STONE BASE

3 **Spread crushed stone** 4in/10cm deep over the subsoil. In large areas, use boards to divide into 13ft/4m sections to allow for expansion joints, without which concrete may crack.

4 **Tamp the crushed stone** down thoroughly with a roller or sturdy wooden post to ensure that there are no voids or air pockets between the crushed stone and subsoil base.

LAYING THE CONCRETE

5 **Tip concrete** into the first section – the depth should be 4in/10cm – and spread level so it is just above the framework. Work into the edges with a spade or masonry trowel.

6 **Use a screed board**, slightly longer than the width of the framework, to compact the concrete with a downward chopping motion. This will remove any air pockets.

7 **Slide the screed** from side to side to level any bumps in the surface, and fill any remaining hollows with fresh concrete. Level the surface one more time, then finish using a float.

8 **Place a protective**, waterproof covering such as plastic sheeting over the concrete and leave for about 10 days. This will trap moisture and help cure the concrete. Remove the framework when the concrete has cured.

PAINTING CONCRETE

Concrete takes one week to one month to set fully, after which it can be painted with a number of different products. Sealant (*right*) does just that, adding an extra layer of protection to the concrete together with a colored pigment. Staining is another method, though you should allow at least 6 weeks from laying fresh concrete before applying the stain. Semi-transparent wood stains take well on concrete. Special concrete paints offer the widest choice of colors, with water-based latex paint being the most effective. Apply 2 or 3 coats.

SEALING CONCRETE

USING DECORATIVE AGGREGATES

Aggregates are usually incorporated to provide cohesion to a concrete mix, but if you choose an attractively colored stone, it can be exposed to create a decorative surface finish that offers an alternative to plain concrete (*see p.43*). Different grades can be used for specific finishes; fine-grade stone, for example, gives a fine-textured surface that is comfortable to walk on. As for plain concrete, aggregates should be laid over a crushed stone base (*see p.42*).

EXPOSED AGGREGATE

YOU NEED:

MATERIALS
• Concrete mix
• Pebbles (or other aggregates, depending on required finish)

TOOLS
• Spade
• Screed board
• Stiff-bristled brush

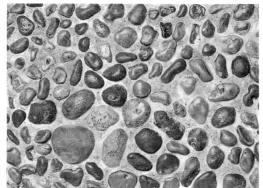

SELECTING A FINISH
Differing grades of gravel or pebbles will give the surface a fine or coarse texture. The color tones of local materials usually blend best.

1 **Mix concrete** and stone thoroughly and, using a spade, lay it onto a firm subbase (*see p.42*). Compact it with a screed board then make it level with the board, but do not finish the surface with a float.

2 **Let the surface** dry for about 6 hours. Remove a thin top layer of concrete by sweeping with a stiff-bristled brush and washing with a fine spray of water. Be sure to leave at least two-thirds of each stone embedded.

3 **Allow concrete** to set for about 36–48 hours. When it is firm, clean any remaining cement residue from the aggregate with a high-pressure water jet, or use a muriatic acid solution and rinse well.

ADDING TEXTURAL DETAIL

If using pebbles or cobblestones for texture, bear in mind that such high-definition surfaces are difficult to walk on. This can be used to positive effect to deter walking on certain areas or, if purely decorative, can be confined to insets or the margins of an area. Pebbles and cobblestones can be set by hand as a decorative surface layer into concrete or mortar. In either case, to ensure that they remain firmly fixed in place, they need to be embedded into the mix to a depth of at least two-thirds their height.

FILLING SLABS WITH PEBBLES
Slabs set on bedding mortar make a secure edge. Set the pebbles into mortar by hand. Once in place, level them by pressing down firmly on a board laid across the slabs.

DECORATIVE MORTAR
Mortar studded with pebbles makes a decorative but secure restraint for widely spaced slabs. Remove the brick spacers before adding the mortar.

LAYING A PEBBLE MOSAIC

Decorative yet durable patterned surfaces can be created by setting pebbles into concrete. Having prepared the base (*see p.36*), lay the edges first. Visually divide the rest of the area into yard/meter-square units and complete each one before moving on to the next. Don't attempt to lay the entire area at once – the concrete will have set hard before you finish.

MOSAIC WORK
When used imaginatively, restrained colors and simple materials can create a pleasing and detailed surface that is both durable and attractive.

STEPPING-STONES

When cement is mixed, the setting process is a chemical reaction between limestone and water, rather than a drying-out process. So concrete can be made in varying consistencies without significantly affecting its durability. If a fine aggregate such as sand is used and it is mixed to a pouring consistency, it can be molded into simple shapes to create stepping-stones that are both stylish and hard-wearing. Apply imaginative decoration to add a highly individual element to your designs. A large, veined leaf has been used here, but a piece of tree bark, seashells, or any other distinctive shape can be used.

MAKING STEPPING-STONES

YOU NEED:

MATERIALS
• Board
• Plastic sheeting
• Plastic mold
• Oil for lubrication
• Sand/cement mix (3 parts sand to 1 part cement)
• Large veined leaf

TOOLS
• Straightedge
• Mixing bucket

1 Choose a mold (here, cut from the top of a large flowerpot) about 2–3in/5–7cm deep. Lubricate the inner surface with oil, and lay it on a sheet of plastic on a flat, level surface or board. Place a leaf – veined surface uppermost – at the base. For best results, use a leaf with pronounced venation.

2 To mix concrete, add one part water to two parts of cement mix. Add concrete dye, if desired, then more water to achieve a pouring consistency. Fill mold to the brim.

3 Level off the excess concrete using a straightedge; drag it across the top of the mold to give an even and level surface. Put to one side to set.

4 When the concrete is firm, dry, and fully set (about 3 days after pouring into the mold), lift the mold and its contents from the plastic sheet and invert it.

5 Apply a little pressure around the edge of the mold, pulling it outward to ease stress on the stone when it is removed. Then slide the mold gently away from the stone.

6 Carefully pick away the leaf from the surface. Small remnants of leaf are best left to wear away naturally; don't try to scratch them off, you may damage the imprint.

7 The finished item is now ready to lay on sand or bedding mortar, as for premade slabs (see p.27). You can adapt the surface decoration to suit the location.

DECORATING CONCRETE

You can decorate concrete with almost any durable material, but you will find that rough-textured pieces will give the most secure bond. Arrange the material in the pattern of your choice on the surface of wet concrete, then push each piece in with a float so that it lies just marginally below surface level. When the concrete is firm, sweep away excess concrete with a stiff-bristled brush and clean with a fine spray of water (see p.11). To remain securely fixed, inlays should be embedded to two-thirds of their depth.

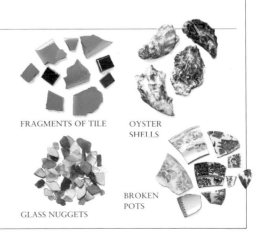

FRAGMENTS OF TILE

OYSTER SHELLS

GLASS NUGGETS

BROKEN POTS

LOOSE SURFACES

LOOSE MATERIALS, whether gravel, stone or bark chippings, are inexpensive, simple to lay, and the ideal choice for areas that incorporate curves – loose materials fill even the most awkward niches without complex cutting. Aesthetically, they create an intermediate texture between hard paving and the softer lines of planting, and they provide an ecologically sound and labor-saving alternative to lawns, needing no feeding, watering, or mowing.

A SIMPLE GRAVELED AREA

If properly laid, gravel is a most versatile and practical medium. It makes a natural link between areas, plants can be planted through it for dramatic or subtle effect, and it permits self-seeders to spread at the edges in pleasing drifts. But for ease of maintenance, comfortable walking, and free passage of wheelbarrows, it is most important to lay gravel on a firm, level, and well-compacted subbase that is cleared of fertile topsoil and free of weeds.

CHOOSING GRAVEL

• Gravels are available in different grades and finishes, obtained as rough chips from parent rock or as dredged, water-worn pebbles. Choose a grade to suit your purpose. Grades less than ¼in/6mm create fine texture but are readily carried into the house on the soles of shoes; any much larger than ½in/12mm are uncomfortable to walk on.
• Buying gravels from a local source can save expense in transportation and may simplify obtaining a color range that blends with the materials used in the house and other garden buildings.

ON THE EDGE
Loose gravel needs a restraining edge, especially where it meets soft surfaces such as lawns. If kicked onto grass, it becomes a hazard as it flies into the air when mown over. It may also damage the mower.

◄ AREA OF TRANSITION *Gravel provides a unifying element between hard paving and soft plants.*

PREPARING THE BASE

YOU NEED:

MATERIALS
• Equal parts small-grade decorative gravel and large-grade compactible gravel
• Bricks and mortar or boards and stakes to make holding edge

TOOLS
• Spade • Rake
• Wheelbarrow
• Power compactor or heavy roller

1 **Having chosen** your site, clear the ground of weeds (it is especially important to eradicate perennial weeds such as bindweed) and remove a 4in/10cm layer of soil from the area. Edge the area with bricks in mortar or treated lumber to keep gravel off the lawn. Alternatively, you can let it merge into a flower bed.

2 **To prepare** the base for graveling, rake the soil level, then fill the excavated area with compactible gravel, or road stone, almost back up to original ground level. Rake the surface completely flat.

3 **Using** a power compactor (which can be rented) or heavy garden roller, compress the base to remove air pockets and thereby provide a stable base. The base needs to be compressed to at least ¾in/2cm below original ground level.

LAYING THE GRAVEL

4 Once you have achieved a firm, compacted base, add the decorative gravel, starting at one side and spreading it as you go.

5 Using a rake, work over the area to create an even surface. The finished level should be just below the edging so that gravel cannot stray onto the lawn. You may then decide to introduce some plants into the area, perhaps to soften edges near beds and borders or for architectural effect.

PLANTING IN GRAVEL

1 Scrape the surface gravel to one side and dig a hole, slightly larger than the plant's rootball, through the gravel base and into the soil below.

2 Fill the hole with compost. Gently tease out the plant's roots, then plant so that it is almost level with the surrounding gravel.

3 Place some of the removed soil around the rootball and firm in. Replace gravel around the stem and under leaves, then water in.

Using Geotextiles

The use of geotextiles, or landscape fabrics, makes laying gravel and other loose surface materials such as bark simple. Geotextiles, made from heat-bonded polypropylene, form a permeable barrier between soil and surface material, helping to suppress weeds yet allowing air and water to pass through. The soil stays healthy and maintenance is kept low. The lightest weights are ideal in gardens and, if properly laid, should last a lifetime.

Laying and Planting Through Geotextile

1 **Remove a layer** of soil 1½in/4–5cm deep, level the area, and lay the geotextile over the surface. Secure the edges with small wire hoops to keep them flat. If gravel butts up to a lawn, install edging boards to keep it in place.

2 **To plant through** the geotextile, make a cross-wise slit big enough to hold the rootball. Dig a planting hole and spread out plant roots. Backfill, firm in, and water. Fold back the geotextile around the stem.

3 **Add the gravel** (or bark). Start at one side and spread it as you go, taking care not to damage plants. A ¾in/2cm layer gives sufficient coverage for most purposes. Finish by leveling with the back of rake.

HOW GEOTEXTILE WORKS

A geotextile fabric greatly extends the life of a gravel, bark, or other loose surface, since it prevents chips from eventually becoming incorporated into the soil or subbase. It makes a light-excluding layer that helps prevent the germination of weed seeds. Because it is permeable to water and air, it does not deprive the soil and plant roots beneath of vital oxygen and moisture as black plastic does; neither does it allow the accumulation of surface water. Applications of fertilizer will be washed down to plant roots. Geotextile also offers the additional benefit of keeping plant roots cool in summer and reducing the depth of freezing in winter.

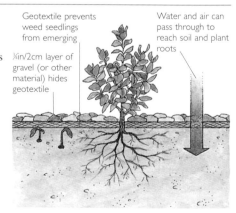

Geotextile prevents weed seedlings from emerging

Water and air can pass through to reach soil and plant roots

¾in/2cm layer of gravel (or other material) hides geotextile

PLANTS FOR GRAVEL

Gravel drains freely and reflects light and heat, so choose plants that thrive in these conditions. Drought-tolerant plants, such as silver-leaved plants from the Mediterranean, are ideal.

Rapid drainage also makes gravel an ideal home for robust alpines. Like plants that prefer dry conditions, these may succumb to winter moisture. Gravel is a perfect foil for architectural plants.

CHOICE PLANTS
Plants with silvery leaves, such as this group of Verbascum, *thrive in gravel; their foliage, especially if felted or hairy, is seen at its best – unsullied by soil and rain splash. The outlines of spiky architectural plants, such as those of many grasses and* Phormium, *stand out beautifully. Self-seeding plants such as fennel (*Foeniculum*) lend informality; be ruthless about pulling out unwanted seedlings, or cut off heads before seeds can disperse.*

GOOD CHOICES FOR GRAVEL

FOR INFORMAL PLANTINGS

Anthemis tinctoria
Centranthus ruber (valerian)
Dictamnus albus
Dryas octopetala, D. drummondii
Foeniculum vulgare 'Purpureum' (bronze-leaved fennel)
Hyssopus officinalis (hyssop)
Lavandula (lavender), many
Lychnis coronaria
Origanum laevigatum
    O. vulgare
Salvia officinalis (sage)

FOR ARCHITECTURAL IMPACT

Acanthus spinosus
Agapanthus, many
Allium, many
Cynara cardunculus (cardoon)
Eremurus robustus
Eryngium, many
Euphorbia, many
Onopordum acanthium
Phormium, many
Verbascum bombyciferum,
    V. 'Cotswold Queen', *V. olympicum*
Yucca flaccida, Y. gloriosa

PATHS THROUGH LOOSE MATERIALS

Areas of gravel or bark chips often benefit from the inclusion of a pathway of firmer, sturdier materials. Stepping-stones of wood, concrete (*see p.46*), or stone, or more heavyweight railroad ties (*see facing page*), look decorative and prevent materials from being scattered or trampled down. In damp, shady woodland, a path like this will reduce the rate at which wood or bark chips are naturally incorporated into the soil beneath.

STEPPING-STONES

A gently curving line of stepping-stones not only provides an irresistible invitation to explore a path, it also gives the opportunity to create patterns that are an integral part of the garden design. When incorporating stepping-stones in a loose surface, the most pleasing results are to be had by selecting materials of a similar nature. Log sections or natural stone are the ideal choice for a woodland floor of bark chips or an area of gravel. Larger units such as railroad ties are ideal for routes that take a lot of traffic, for instance a path that links two separate but frequently used garden areas.

MAKING THE PATH SAFE

• Lay small units on a firm subbase, and bed them on sand or mortar to keep them secure and prevent gravel from working its way underneath and lifting the stepping-stone.
• To avoid tripping, keep the surface of stepping-stones or ties as level as possible with the surrounding loose materials.
• Treat wooden materials with preservative before laying.
• Make sure that stepping-stones have a non-slip surface; wood surfaces can be made safe by applying wire netting (*see p.69*).

OBVIOUS ROUTE
Light-colored stepping-stones show up well against bark chips, reducing the risk of stumbling against the edges of the stones.

TEXTURAL HARMONY
Cross-sections from the trunk of a tree make a harmonious path across a floor of dried leaves in a shady woodland area.

LAYING A PATH OF RAILROAD TIES

1 **Dig out foundations** to create a firm, level base. The foundation trench needs to be slightly deeper than the height of the ties to allow for a base layer of sharp sand.

2 **Bed the ties** on the sand in the desired pattern. Firm down so that they are level and flush with surrounding surfaces. Lift carefully to avoid hurting your back.

3 **When the ties** are in position, fill in the gaps with excavated soil. Bed securely by firming well with your heels. In dry weather, water the soil to aid compaction.

4 **Top off with gravel** to cover compacted soil. Use a heavy roller to firm it between the ties; make sure the finished surface is even and level with the ties.

5 **The finished** surface is not only practical, durable, and easily negotiable, it blends perfectly with its surroundings. Ties are ideal for making a wide but curving path; the repetition of strong horizontal lines defines the way and leads the eye onward.

WOODEN DECKING

WOOD IS ONE OF THE WARMEST and most natural of materials to use
outdoors. Though long used in building, when used for decking it is one
of the most modern elements in garden design. Infinitely versatile, you can let
its warmth shine through, or stain or paint it to suit your taste. It is equally at
home in situations as diverse as coastal gardens, stylish urban courtyards, and
in wilder, more naturalistic, rural settings.

MAKING A SIMPLE DECKING PLATFORM

Constructing an area of decking, such
as the platform below and on the next
page, requires little in the way of
building skills and no carpentry skills
at all. Concrete blocks are used for the
foundations, and laying the boards
involves no woodwork joints. This
construction method would suit a
small patio or slightly raised boardwalks
(*p.63*). Deeper, sturdier joists would
allow you to increase the height.

USING WOOD OUTDOORS

• Use only lumber that has been pressure-
treated with preservative to extend its
outdoor life. Most processes give the surface
a greenish tinge. This will not affect the
finished color if you intend to stain it, but if
you want the warmth of natural wood, look
for special landscaping lumber that has been
treated with colorless preservatives.

• Tropical hardwoods, such as iroko, combine
great beauty with durability and, while very
expensive, last a lifetime. Be sure that they
come from sustainable forestry sources.

DESIGN AND CONSTRUCTION
This 8ft/2.5m square platform uses a building method (see
next page) that makes it easy to adjust size and shape. Tiny
gaps between the boards allow the wood to swell when wet.

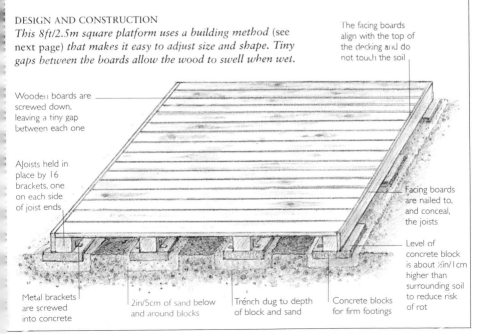

The facing boards
align with the top of
the decking and do
not touch the soil

Wooden boards are
screwed down,
leaving a tiny gap
between each one

Joists held in
place by 16
brackets, one
on each side
of joist ends

Facing boards
are nailed to,
and conceal,
the joists

Level of
concrete block
is about ½in/1cm
higher than
surrounding soil
to reduce risk
of rot

Metal brackets
are screwed
into concrete

2in/5cm of sand below
and around blocks

Trench dug to depth
of block and sand

Concrete blocks
for firm footings

◄ STAGGERED DECKING *Wooden platforms float through an established planting.*

PLANNING THE SITE

YOU NEED:

MATERIALS
- 16 boards, 8ft/2.5m× 6in/15cm×1in/2.5cm
- 4 wooden joists, 8ft/2.5m×4in/10cm× 4in/10cm
- 4 facing boards, 2 measuring 8ft/2.5m× 4in/10cm×¾in/2cm and 2 8ft4in/2.54m× 4in/10cm×¾in/2cm
- 4 55lb/25kg bags sand
- 12 concrete blocks
- 16 metal 2in/5cm angle brackets
- 2in/5cm nails/screws
- Wallplugs

TOOLS
- Spade • Level
- Framing square
- Maul • Drill and bits

1 Measure out the decking area, using 4 boards laid out in a square. Check that the corners form right angles by using a framing square. The marked-out area will be 6in/15cm larger than the desired 8ft/2.5m square platform, but the extra space will be needed for digging the foundation trenches.

2 Mark out the boundaries of the work area by drawing the blade of a spade along the outside edges of the boards. Take care not to nudge the boards out of position before you have finished marking out the square. Put 3 of the boards to one side until later.

3 Lay the joists, parallel to each other within the square so that they are evenly spaced. Use one 8ft/2.5m board to ensure that the first and last joists lie flush with the ends of the plank. Mark out a 6in/15cm wide border around each joist to determine where the trenches should be.

PREPARING THE BASE OF THE DECKING

1 **Dig the trenches.** They should be 1½in/4cm deeper than the depth of the concrete blocks. Line the base of each trench with sand, then firm it by treading it down and level it so that it forms a 2in/5cm deep bed.

2 **Lay the concrete blocks,** 3 to a trench, placing one block at each end of a trench and one in the center. The blocks should stand above the soil by ½in/1cm so that the joists will not come into contact with the soil.

3 **Check the level** of the blocks, both along and across the trenches, using a board and a level. If necessary, adjust the level of any block: lift it and add a little more sand or gently knock it down with the handle of your maul. Check the levels again.

4 **Backfill each trench** around the blocks with more sand, treading it down as you go to create a firm base. If not compacted, the sand bed will settle naturally, the blocks will shift or sink, and the decking will warp. Level off the sand so that it is flush with the surface of the soil.

CONSTRUCTING THE PLATFORM

1 **Lay the joists** across the concrete blocks, then center them on the blocks. Check again that the first and last joists are exactly 8ft/2.5m apart, using one of the boards. The ends of all the joists should also be in line.

2 **Secure the joists** in place using the metal brackets, on either side of each end of the joists. Place each bracket in position and mark the screw holes, one on the joist and one on the supporting block. Remove the bracket.

3 **Drill the screw holes** to a depth of 2in/5cm, using a suitably sized masonry bit for the concrete and a wooden drill bit for the joist. Insert wallplugs in the concrete. Screw the bracket in place. Each joist requires 4 brackets.

4 **Put the first board** into place. Lay it across all 4 joists so that its edge sits flush with the ends of the joists. Drill 2 screw holes per joist, drilling through the board and about ¼in/6mm into the joist below. Then screw the board in place. For a finer finish, use a special bit to countersink the screws.

5 **Position all the boards** across the joists, leaving a tiny space of ¼in/6mm between each board. The last board should sit flush with the ends of the joists. Check that the boards are evenly spaced, then screw into place as for the first board (*see step 4*). The gaps between the boards allow the wood to swell when wet without warping.

6 **Fit the facing boards**, nailing them into place along the edges of the joists. Each board needs at least 4 nails to hold it. Secure 2 8ft/2.5m facing boards across the ends of the joists, then fit 2 8ft4in/2.54m boards along the length of the joists, so that they overlap the first 2 boards neatly at each corner. Trim the corners, if needed.

RAISING DECKING LEVELS

Laying decking at different levels is one of the simplest ways of introducing a visually interesting change of height to an otherwise level garden. The simplest construction technique is to screw or bolt a second tier onto the first. If using the above method, run the second set of joists at right angles to those used for the first tier, to give extra strength. The technique of altering the direction of the parallel slats lends an extra dimension of interest; it can also be used to emphasize and warn of a change in level. Diagonal slats are particularly effective.

NEW HEIGHTS
A second layer of decking gives an elevated view over the area. When the slats are laid diagonally, they give a sense of movement.

FINISHING THE WOOD

Since the range of wood finishes is now so extensive, check with your supplier that the one you have chosen suits the job at hand. Pressure-treated lumber needs only occasional treatment with preservative, but you may still wish to apply color for decoration or to offset the dulling effects of weather.

ADDING COLOR

There are two basic ways of coloring wood: with paint or with stain. Exterior wood paints are opaque, with a "microporous" finish that allows wood to breathe and helps prevent peeling or cracking. Wood stains are translucent and darken and/or color wood. They penetrate the surface, allowing the grain to show through. Exterior formulas often include preservative. All surfaces must be clean, dry, and dust-free before treating. Before painting, wood will need priming and undercoating. Apply paint or stain with a good-quality brush in the direction of the grain.

NATURAL SHADES
Preservatives combined with stain are available in a good range of natural wood colors.

TEMPTING COLORS
Wood dyes in a water, oil, or solvent base provide a wide choice of colors. Oil-based ones are the easiest to apply: they dry slowly. If water-based, color intensity can be enhanced by the addition of pigments.

USING TILED PANELS FOR TEXTURE

Prefab panels, some of which have a nonslip finish, come in a range of patterns perfect for introducing changes of texture. Use a checkerboard design, for instance, or create your own larger and bolder version from panels of parallel slats. When laying prefab panels, take accurate measurements and space the joists carefully so that the panels are securely supported.

SCREWING IN PLACE
Brass screws and hardware are best, followed closely by galvanized. Since they do not rust, they will not make stains on surrounding wood and can be removed if repairs are needed.

CHECKERBOARD　　HERRINGBONE　　PARALLEL SLATS　　ANGLED　　PARALLEL-JOINTED

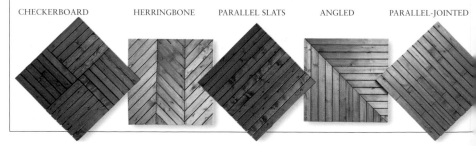

BOARDWALKS AND BRIDGES

Narrow decking platforms may be used as boardwalks and simple bridges. There is no need to lay foundations for a boardwalk; simply lay the constructed platforms on level ground and set them in position by driving in short fence posts at 3ft/1m intervals on either side. A bridge will need foundations; for safety reasons it must be at least 24in/60cm wide and have a span of no more than 8ft/2.5m. Cut the joists and cross-boards to the required length and width before laying foundations.

A NONSLIP BOARDWALK
Wood becomes slippery when wet. Fine wire mesh nailed firmly over the boards makes an unobtrusive nonslip surface. Scrub the wood regularly to keep it free of moss and algae.

MAKING A BRIDGE

YOU NEED:

MATERIALS
- 8 pieces rough lumber
- 4 55lb/25kg bags concrete
- 2 wooden joists
- 4 brackets (5in/13cm) and 8 2in/5cm bolts and nuts
- Cross-boards
- 2in/5cm, 8-gauge screws

TOOLS
- Spade, straightedge, level, screwdriver, drill

1 **Construct the foundations** for the bridge ends. Dig 2 holes 8–12in/20–30cm wider than the bridge, 8in/20cm across, 4in/10cm deep. Use rough lumber and bricks to make rectangular forms. Fill with concrete, using a straightedge and level to check both blocks are level.

2 **Set the joists** across the blocks at the required width apart and 4–6in/10–15cm in from the edges. Mark through the brackets where to put the bolts. Embed in the concrete with 1in/2.5cm of their screw ends exposed.

3 **Bolt on the brackets** when the concrete is dry. Remove the molds and screw the joists to the brackets. Put any liner under the bridge. Lay the cross-boards across the joists and secure in place as for decking (*see p.61*).

GETTING DOWN TO BASICS

MATERIALS

FOR MOST GARDENERS, the extensive choice of building materials available can be daunting – how do you select the right materials for the task at hand, and how do you estimate quantities? In recent years, builders' supply stores have made great efforts in the field of customer service and have become a good source of expert advice. But it helps enormously if you are familiar with the common materials and the terms used to describe them.

PAVING AND HARD SURFACES

Apart from cost, the intended use of a surface is a prime consideration. The greater the load, the stronger the subbase and more durable the finish must be. For most garden surfaces, firm subsoil or a 4in/10cm layer of crushed stone topped with 2in/5cm of sand makes a good subbase. Areas that must bear the weight of vehicles need a subbase of 4in/10cm of compacted stone with a further 4in/10cm of concrete as a laying surface. Always seek expert advice before embarking on more ambitious projects.

PAVING UNITS

Paving slabs: cast or pressed concrete, or reconstituted or real stone, in a range of colors, sizes, and textures.
Bricks: wide range but of variable durability. Must be frostproof and nonslip.
Clay pavers: small, durable units, very similar to bricks, for bedding on sand, in a wide range of shapes, sizes, and colors.
Setts: usually of granite; can last for centuries. Available in a range of shapes, sizes, and colors.
Terracotta tiles: beautiful but porous and will crack if exposed to severe cold. Some may be slippery.

SURFACE FINISHES *Ensure that surface materials are totally weather-resistant, durable enough for the job at hand, and provide a safe, non-slip walking surface when laid.*

TERRACOTTA TILES

PAVING SLAB

GRANITE SETTS

LOOSE MATERIALS

Loose materials are used as decorative surface finishes and as aggregates in cement mixes; the grade (and cost) determines use. In general, the larger the grade and more decorative the appearance, the higher the cost. For decorative uses, size is important; it dictates how easily negotiable the surface will be. Use pea gravel or other decorative stones for walking on; use cobblestones for decoration and to restrict free passage.

COBBLESTONES AND PEBBLES   GRAVEL

LOOSE MATERIALS

Aggregate: this term usually refers to materials such as gravel and other decorative stones that are incorporated into concrete for strength or for a more interesting surface appearance. Avoid using grades larger than ¾in/20mm to reduce the chance of difficulties when using hand tools.

Cobblestones: refers to large, rounded, naturally occurring stones or to cut pieces of stone used for surfaces or edges.

Crushed stone: sometimes called roadstone, this is ground-up, washed, graded stone most often used as a subbase.

Gravel: this refers to small pebbles (such as pea gravel) or to some grades of crushed stone such as compactible gravel, which is made up of larger pieces of stone combined with a range of smaller pieces grading down to dustlike particles, used as a subbase.

CONCRETE AND MORTAR

Concrete and mortar have different components and are used for different purposes (*see box, below right*). Bedding mortar is a mix of 1 part cement: 5 parts sharp sand. Masonry mortar is a mix of 1 part masonry cement: 3 parts soft sand.

BUILDER'S SAND   CEMENT POWDER

DRY MORTAR MIX

WET MORTAR MIX

For concrete for wall footings, foundations, and bases for precast paving, mix 1 part cement, 2½ parts sand, and 3½ parts ¾in/20mm aggregate. For poured concrete: 1 part cement, 1½ parts sharp sand, and 2½ parts ¾in/20mm aggregate. All parts are by volume.

USEFUL TERMS

Cement: a gray powder containing limestone. Mixed with water, it reacts to form the bonding agent in mortar and concrete.

Concrete: a mix of coarse aggregate, sand, cement, and water that forms a hard-setting building or surface material.

Mortar: a mix of cement, sand, and water for bonding bricks, stones, or concrete slabs. Bedding mortar is used for laying and jointing pavers; it is made with sharp sand rather than soft sand. Dry-mix mortar is a stiff mix with less water used to fill paving joints. Masonry mortar, made with soft sand and masonry cement, is used for brickwork.

Sand: soft or builders' sand is fine-grade and salt-free and is used for mortar mixes. Sharp sand is coarser; some grades used for concrete are sometimes called concreting sand.

ORDERING AND QUANTITIES

When ordering materials, check transportation and delivery arrangements, and ask about the supplier's return policy; most reputable businesses will accept returns of unused bagged materials if unopened. If you are using reclaimed materials from a salvage yard, however, you are more likely to be buying unique lots of material, and their repeat availability may be limited. In this case, you need to make a careful estimate of your requirements to make sure that you have enough materials to complete the task.

CALCULATING QUANTITIES

Most reputable suppliers are happy to advise on the quantities of materials you will need to complete your job, provided that you tell them clearly the overall dimensions of the project in hand. To calculate volumes needed for regular areas, simply multiply length by width by depth. For irregular areas, draw out the site on a piece of graph paper using a scale of one square to each square foot or yard/meter. Count all the complete squares and any that are more than one-third full. Multiply this figure by the depth to find the final volume.

ESTIMATING
QUANTITIES
This 50lb/25kg bag of sand spread out to a 2in/5cm layer yields a surprisingly small area, 30×30in/ 75×75cm, in extent. It shows how difficult it can be for the inexperienced to calculate quantities, so don't be afraid to ask your supplier for expert advice.

DELIVERY AND STORAGE

For most bulky building materials, suppliers will deliver straight to your door. If possible, try to arrange for delivery direct to the site to minimize the heavy labor of transporting them there later. You also need to give some forethought to storing the materials, since the volumes involved are likely to be considerable.

If you intend to lay large areas of concrete, having premixed concrete delivered makes the job a lot quicker and easier as long as there is easy access for large vehicles. The supplier will calculate volumes needed if given site dimensions and information about the intended use and load bearings of the surface, but the site needs to be well prepared in advance.

THINGS TO CONSIDER

• By their very nature, building materials are often high volume, so consider carefully where they can be stored safely until you use them. Some items, such as cement, need to be kept dry until used and will need a covered storage area or plastic sheeting.

• Moving building materials is heavy work, so try to recruit a team of helpers. This – and advanced preparation – is vital when taking delivery of premixed concrete that must be dealt with quickly before it sets.

• In an ideal world, materials are delivered directly to the site, but if, for example, you live in an urban area, easy access may not be possible. If you need to carry materials through the house, take steps to protect interior walls and surfaces.

TOOLS FOR THE JOB

USING THE CORRECT TOOLS for the job always makes the task easier. Some simple items, such as a framing square and float, can be made at home, while others, such as a builder's screed (used for striking off to create a level surface) can effectively be substituted with a board. For smaller hardware, such as masonry trowels, where quality and durability is less important than it is for professional use, the outlay need only be minimal; you can get away with the cheapest version.

INVESTING IN TOOLS

For some tasks, high-quality tools really make a difference to the finished article, and this is especially true of measuring tools such as tapes and levels. Accurate measurement is fundamental to a professional finish, so it is well worth investing in the best you can afford. With proper care, they'll last a lifetime, and you will undoubtedly find them useful for a variety of other projects. To ensure that tools perform and last well, they must be well maintained. This is most important for tools used for concrete and mortar work, since these materials set hard if not cleaned off immediately after use. Metal surfaces should be wiped with an oily rag and stored in dry conditions to prevent rusting.

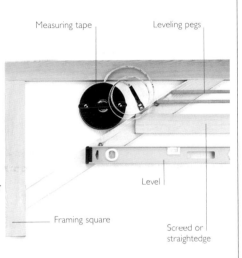

Measuring tape

Leveling pegs

Level

Framing square

Screed or straightedge

RENTING SPECIALIZED EQUIPMENT

The heavy manual labor of mixing concrete and compacting subbases is only for the fit and strong, but specialized rental businesses carry a wide range of machinery to lighten the load. Some of the most useful items are stone or slab cutters, cement mixers, and power compactors. A good specialist can offer advice on the most suitable equipment for the job at hand, and most rent by the full day. It is most important, especially if you're unfamiliar with machinery, that you get a demonstration of how it works and how to use it safely; some of the best suppliers produce operating and safety literature. They may also supply any necessary protective gear, such as goggles and ear protectors.

POWER COMPACTOR
A mechanical compactor shortens the work of preparing subbases and laying flexible pavers and is especially useful for large areas.

Maintenance and Safety

Statistically, outdoor accidents account for a significant proportion of home-based incidents, and the potential for serious injury increases where you are using heavy machinery. Take all sensible precautions, and check that all power tools are in good repair. If you are unfamiliar with a tool or piece of machinery, ask advice when buying or renting, or contact the manufacturer.

Protect Yourself

A sturdy pair of gloves is essential when dealing with mortar and concrete; the lime content can burn if it comes into contact with skin. Always use goggles to protect your eyes if dealing with loose materials, and ear protectors when using equipment such as compactors and cement mixers. Wear close-fitting clothing when using any machine with moving parts, and take special care to keep head, limbs, and shovels clear when loading cement mixers. Even the professionals use kneelers or cushioned, waterproof knee pads to make groundwork more comfortable.

KNEELERS

GLOVES

EAR PROTECTORS

GOGGLES

LIFTING CORRECTLY
To protect your back, never lift by bending from the waist. Use the strength of your legs to lift the load, and carry heavy items close to your body. Don't overestimate your capabilities – remember that a load shared is a load halved.

INCORRECT LIFTING STANCE

CORRECT LIFTING STANCE

USING ELECTRICAL TOOLS

• The safe use of electrical tools depends on the observation of a few simple rules. One of the most important is the use of a ground fault interrupt (GFI) device, also called a ground fault circuit interrupter (GFCI). If not already fitted, attach a GFI adapter between plug and socket.

• Do not use an electric tool during or just after rain; this may cause electrical hazards.

• Always disconnect the power supply before adjusting, cleaning, or inspecting a tool, and never touch a severed or damaged cord before disconnecting from the source.

• Use cords that are only as long as necessary; trailing cords are potentially hazardous. Extension cords should have the same number of wires as the tool and must be grounded.

KEEPING SURFACES SAFE

With the exception of graveled areas, hard surfaces that are exposed to wet weather – especially in areas that are shaded or walked over infrequently – are likely to build up a slippery layer of mosses, algae, or fungi. They can be removed with a stiff brush using a scrub of sharp sand and water or treated with muriatic acid. Wooden surfaces need regular maintenance. Once a year, check for splits and cracks and replace any damaged members. On wooden surfaces, fungal growths are inevitable in damp climates; they can be washed with a stiff brush and a mild solution of household bleach, or treated with commercial fungicides. Small units, such as wooden stepping-stones, can be brushed clean with a wire brush. When using chemical cleaners, make sure that they are suitable for use with plants, or take steps to protect them. This is especially important where surfaces are near to water; plant and animal pond life is extremely vulnerable to chemicals.

GETTING A GRIP

In damp or shaded areas, a covering of wire mesh will ensure a nonslip surface. Initially unattractive, it soon weathers into invisibility.

PREVENT SLIPPERY WOOD

• Nail chicken wire firmly in place onto wooden decking or stepping-stones to provide an unobtrusive, nonslip surface.
• Keep wood underfoot clean and free of algae by scouring regularly with a wire brush.
• If using chemical cleaning agents, make sure that they are safe to use near plants.

CONTROLLING WEEDS

You can control weeds on paving surfaces by hand-weeding or using an herbicide, preferably a systemic one. Herbicides can be applied using a back-pack sprayer for large areas. On smaller areas, it is practical to use a dribble bar. Where ornamental plants are present, a spot-weeder may be your best weapon of choice.

WEEDS IN GRAVEL

Use a liquid herbicide to treat large areas Reserve a clearly marked watering can or sprayer for dispensing herbicides.

ONE-TO-ONE ACTION

Spot-weeding is essential if weeds coexist with ornamentals. Use a weed wand or apply herb-icide with a brush reserved for the purpose.

INDEX

ACKNOWLEDGMENTS

Editorial contributors
Linden Hawthorne, Geoff Stebbings

Picture research Anna Grapes

Special photography Peter Anderson

Illustrations Karen Cochrane

Index Ella Skene

DK Publishing would like to thank:
All staff at the RHS, in particular Susanne
Mitchell, Barbara Haynes, and Karen Wilson
at Vincent Square; Annelise Evans, Candida
Frith-Macdonald, Phil Hunt, and Lesley
Malkin for editorial assistance. Also Ken
Selody II of Atlock Farm for his assistance
with terminology and techniques.

American Horticultural Society
Visit AHS at www.ahs.org or call them at
1-800-777-7931 ext. 10. Membership benefits
include *The American Gardener* magazine,
free admission to flower shows, the free seed
exchange, book services, and the Gardener's
Information Service.

Photography
The publisher would also like to thank the
following for their kind permission to
reproduce their photographs:
(key: t=top, c=center, b=bottom, l=left,
r=right, fj=front jacket, bj=back jacket)

DIY Photo Library: 67cr
Garden Picture Library: 9tl, 13tr; Brian Carter
9crb, 21crb, 28tl; Christi Carter 21tr; David
Askham 22br; Gary Rogers 22tr, 40; Howard
Rice 69tl; Jerry Pavia 8bl; Joanne Pavia 11t;
John Glover 13tl, 14cr, 18br; Lamontagne
16br, 56; Philippe Bonduel 54bl; Ron
Sutherland 14b, 16bl, 18cl, 20br, 22bl, 29tl,
30tr, 60tl; Tim MacMillan 34
John Glover: 32cr
Jerry Harpur: 10b, 41bl, 45bl
Clive Nichols: 19t, 48; design: Jean Bishop
7br, 12br, 15tl; Green Farm Plants/Piet Oudolf
53c; Save the Children – Chelsea 1991 28bl;
Elizabeth Whiting & Associates: 6; design:
J King 24

Jacket: commissioned photography with the
exception of **Garden Picture Library:** fj bl;
Ron Sutherland fj cl, bj c; Jerry Pavia bj tl;
John Glover bj tr; **Clive Nichols:** design Jean
Bishop fj tl; **Steve Wooster:** fj l